ALL RED
a collection of poetry

Poetry by Anna Casamento Arrigo
inspired by the artwork of Gregory Anthony Stone

Copyright © 2014 Anna Casamento Arrigo
All rights reserved
First Edition

FULTON BOOKS, INC.
New York, NY

First originally published by Fulton Books, Inc. 2014

ISBN 978-1-63338-002-8 (pbk)
ISBN 978-1-63338-003-5 (digital)

Printed in the United States of America
Artwork/Imagery: All rights reserved to
Gregory Anthony Stone gstone1950@optimum.net

Dedication

For all artists, writers, musicians, and poets who inspire us to
express our own emotions through their creations.

A special dedication is also given to
Gregory Anthony Stone, the artist, who inspired
some of the poems in this collection and
whose work demonstrates passion, depth, and pathos
and its effect on the individual in a variety of ways.

All Red, Gregory Anthony Stone, 2013

ALL RED

I am caught in the Polar Region of this great earth
Perhaps, some have visited there,
and noticed the fissure that separates one icy layer from another.
It belies explanation, though many have given it a name
I choose to question all those names.
While I slide and skate upon one side
My laughter and joy echoes through the great Buddhist Mountain
So I have come to learn and so it is
The Mountain of Congregation.
Some days it is not so and some days it is here that my thoughts come together
A baptism into happiness
On the days when my body, soul, and mind take me to
That almost fissure
That the greatest anomaly exists.
All Red and nothing more, my hell
But, it is not part of who I am, I believe,
though I have been told it is.
What's in you?
Follow your heart!
Oops...
I've crossed that almost imperceptible fissure
Though, at present, it is not so imperceptible to me.
I crossed, fully urged by those voices, I sometimes, consider my friends
Though I know full well they may not be.
They exist only in my mind and I am totally aware
I am happy and comforted
Knowing they will not make their presence known to the
Outer world...others
Still, I listen, sometimes, when my feet take me to the
other side of the Polar Region.

And it is here that I find the All Red of it.
Hell and heaven disconnected by that fissure
That I, through no will of my own, have crossed.
My feet sinking deep and deeper still
An inescapable truth.
My feet leaving small prints that serve to remind…
Not just me, but, all those around me as well.
Delusions all?
Like the Easter Bunny waiting for the ice to melt
So that his goodies may be delivered to waiting hands
Mine included.
Fear me not, I shall not harm you.
All Red is mine and mine alone, just as yours belongs to you alone.
Today is a day when the adult world shatters that
innocence of childhood.
And our Muses would have it otherwise.
Not today.
Some days, I find my only companion is All Red
And my mind plays fisticuffs with the greatest joke of all…
Depression.
I run still trying desperately trying to cross that fissure that,
sometimes, is not so insignificant
At All!
My art, the music, sometimes, most times, all the time,
becomes my solace
And for those days, when the melting side of that Polar Ice is of
No consequence
It is enough.

Final Viewing, Bury the Dead, Gregory Anthony Stone, 2000

FINAL VIEWING- BURY THE DEAD

I've watched you looking at me blankly
Wrapped deep in thought
While I hunger for your touch.
I am dying in the emptiness of my white world
Waiting, wanting your touch.
Fill me with your words.
Give me birth
As a mother does her child
A mother who will touch, caress, kiss the innocence born.
Give me birth.
Rise from your melancholy chair
That has been crushed long enough.
Release your words, your vision, and your emotions
I will take them willingly.
Caress me with your strokes.
I can wait no longer, neither can you.
Fill my void of white with your varied brushes
Covered with the vibrant colors of the sun
The moon
The earth
Life...I need life...I need your life.
Relieve my pain and I shall relieve yours.
Just caress me.
We are lovers after all
And when others do not see that affection, that passion
That holds us forever together
It will not matter.
Just touch me, feel my gentleness surround and comfort you
As you will comfort me with your gentleness
Do not think about the should-haves, the could-haves, the might-have-beens...
Just touch me, caress me, fill me with your passion.
Allow me to capture your vision, your thoughts, your words
I promise I shall hold them lovingly forever.
Forever, because we are lovers, after all.

Pygmalion, Gregory Anthony Stone, 1998

PYGMALION

A sculpture, I have come to life
Falling in love
With myself, a false love
I have learned, and continuing learning, that
There is no greater love than that…
And while I sit looking out the window pane
To all those wandering seeking shelter from the downpour
They do not notice the one who sits
Crying tears
That flow and are caught by the white sill beneath
Pain!
Love…even of, or for, myself does not exist.
I am alone, watching, crying my tears of sadness
Knowing, but for those tears, my heart would burst.
I do not care to travel to India
Any change, like here, now, will not alter my life.
I shall leave you as I find you
On your own
Like me and…
The gentile manners and grander life
Will make no difference.
My solitude so great…
It is my pain and mine alone.
So continue seeking shelter from the downpour
Of tears that rain from the skies
Find me, consume me
Love that could be
Love that has yet to find me
I have been wooed before and probably
Shall be again.

Lies upon lies
And I, still crying, sobbing out behind the window... pain
Will never be misguided yet again.
You spoke of beauty
But it only served to remind me of the remnants of my past.
It will pass
Finding me unchanged.
Leave me unnoticed, brooding, silent
Clinging to tomorrow
When the sun will shine
And may find me in the fields
Gathering colorful flowers
Then and only then will change come.
Yes, pass by my window, ignore my tears
It will not change how I feel at this moment
I will allow my tears to flow effortlessly
And hit the sill
It is quite familiar and my friend
My strength...
And somewhere deep within I know even this to be transient
But it is here with my friend that I have chosen to sit
As I have so many times before.
It is here that I shall await the passing of the rain...
The pain
For tomorrow will come and find me
Gathering flowers in the field.

The Desert Boot, Gregory Anthony Stone, 1968

THE DESERT BOOT

Heavily my foot lands upon the sands of the Sahara-
In its massiveness, it is the largest, after all,
I shall find my way.
I shall seek the oasis where Dromedary camels come to rest-
If only for a short while
Taking in water that will hold them over
Many days.
I shall drink...I shall drink
And in doing so, I shall come alive
Again.
It is real, that oasis, after all
And while the Desert Boot weighs heavily
Upon my foot-I'll ignore the discomfort it brings
And move on
Further into Africa searching out
The beautiful flat-footed Addax
And make my way along the sandy landscape of the Sahara's.
I shall not be easy prey for the poachers
Who may seek me out-
I shall outlast them all-
They will not feast on my meat and...
Rip my leather.
I am stronger, more cunning than they realize...I will not be easy
prey.
the Desert Boot helping me along
Farther into the vast Sahara
Greeting the horned viper, whose horns protect its
Eyes
Against the sand-
Camouflage
Though I do not expect it to be so
As I travel in the daylight-

the Desert Boot, pinching, weighing heavily-
I shall ignore the pain of it-
And farther into the great Sahara I shall go-
Still greeting, with the Desert Boot, a Dorcas gazelle,
That has found some leaves from trees and bushes
And watch it for a while-
I shall eat the fruit of the trees-
If it will share-
And take berries from the bushes
Should some be there.
The farther I traverse the vast, relentless miles of sand,
The heavier the Desert Boot
Like the noose that held me in check
As I made my way down the cement walks
Of bustling, chaotic, frantic streets
Squeezing myself into overcrowded subways
That took the ghost-like and worn faces
Of people, a mingling of smells, and the grinding
Halt of squeaky wheels here and there
Marking, announcing exits, my exit.
There is no oasis in the city
No respite for me and my heavy Desert Boot.
So I travel and explore.
Watching, just watching a monitor lizard
Who so reminds me of cold-blooded souls
In that subway or frantically scampering to
I know not where
Nor do I care.
I so prefer to sit upon the sand and
Watch, just watch as the monitor lizard,
Out in the extreme heat of the great Sahara
And I am unafraid...I am unafraid
I do not wish to fight
And the basking lizard, like so many
On those chaotic city streets

Will look upon me pityingly as I sit,
the Desert Boot reminding me of pain, restrictions,
Frantic, hurried life along the treeless city pavement.
Yes, I shall sit.
Released from a self-imposed captivity of heart, body, and soul.
I too, like the lizard, sometimes chooses, shall flee.
And the Desert Boot, I come to realize
Will continue to pinch, cramp, and remind me-
I so prefer to travel, most times, alone
Wrapped in my own thoughts
Thoughts that would not come so easily
Good thoughts
Thoughts that enabled, encouraged me to find
My oasis-
Where I may drink to satisfy my soul
Then, and only then, shall I know
Contentment and renew my need to create
Express my thoughts using vibrant colors
That reveal my those thoughts, my soul
In agony and joy
And I shall overcome the reminders the Desert Boot offers.
And if I choose to bury my head in the sand, like the Ostrich
That has found me-
At this oasis-
I will watch it graze on grass and bushes
And the occasional small animal
That may come too close-
But it will serve to remind me
That I too may feed and nourish my soul, my heart, my mind and...
That I have greater strength
Than the predators that scamper, run in chaos
Along the busy city streets,
Who do not welcome the possibility of reaching
Their oasis-
Greeting others, welcoming their habits, their needs
You see, they do not own the Desert Boot!

Abandon Us Laughing Friend, Gregory Anthony Stone,

ABANDON US LAUGHING FRIEND

In our hours, days of turmoil, angst, and pain
You are there…you are there.
So little do you understand that our illness, my disease must overcome your laughter
Your reminders.
My putty arms and legs are mine
Like so many others we…
Black and grey your laughter is all that has become our reality
Replacing the sunlight that once warmed our being…
Remember, laughing friend, you who now are its keeper
And so, we look to the shadow
You, our laughing friend who has taken that sunlight
And replaced it with a dark, grey etching that dances in our mind
Lyrics embedded in the walls and encased waiting your return
Our laughing friend.
"I must go. I must go. It is late. It is too late. I cannot stay. I must go."
But you do not.
Refusing to take your laughter with you.
Abandon Us Our Laughing Friend!
And, in our minds, we shall find solace somehow
It shall come.
Then my friend, in moments of distress…
That it will wrap us in its arms and sing a lullaby.
This much we know, it will sing us a lullaby
And we shall sleep curled up and smiling,
And in moments of solitude
We may give thought to our laughing friend
Long since gone, never to return

And do not encourage us with our self-pity
That ebbs and flows in tides
Of our emotions…play not on the merry-go-round
In our mind…now, we shall ask and give you permission
To Abandon Us My Laughing Friend!

Today Walk, Tomorrow Climb A Tree, Gregory Anthony Stone, 201

TODAY WALK TOMORROW CLIMB A TREE

A stroke...time
I am an infant trying to turn from my stomach to my back
Over and over again.
I am a toddler learning words, babbles at first, but trying just the same.
I am taking my first steps, faltering, falling down on my bottom...
Trying over and over again...
First steps, second steps, and so on
My parents laughing and clapping their hands
Their outstretched arms urging me on.
A stroke...time.
I walked today...first steps...more followed
A cane assisting my steps, enabling my balance, but I walked.
Today Walk Tomorrow Climb A Tree.
I mouthed words, the order of things, even for us toddlers, is never the same
Words that do not sound right
Words that get caught, stuck somewhere between my brain and mouth
Words that were once so familiar they rolled off my tongue with ease.
Those same words that I now find awkward and uncomfortable
I find myself questioning whether or not those words make sense
If they came out with the appropriate stress,
The right word...the one that rolled around in my head
Just waiting...they often sounded so different than they had before.
A stroke...time.
Today Walk Tomorrow Climb a Tree.
Turning over and over again...

Walking, faltering in my gait, unsteady
Left leg choosing not to cooperate fully
Left arm solidly affixed to my side
Not realizing or accepting that it is still part of me!
A stroke…time.
I practice all those things the toddler in me had mastered just yesterday
Or so it seems.
Betrayal, Anger, Grief, Acceptance…
Today Walk, Tomorrow Climb a Tree.
And so my weary body, an infant once again, a toddler
Will…
A stroke…time.
I so long to climb a tree just as I did just yesterday
Or so it seems.
I'd like to climb a tree, any tree, with no purpose
Other than I can!
Acceptance and the reality that is a new me
The same but different…
Remembering details, experiences, both good and bad
Finding their way from my brain to my lips,
Slowly, and with practice, they do.
Jumbled, awkward, mispronounced but they do.
Do not ask what day it is
Do not ask what I ate for breakfast, or lunch, or dinner
A stroke…time
Do not ask what I read, what I learned, what I understood
The plot, the setting, the theme, the characters
And, most especially, the author
He is anonymous, this I decided.
A stroke…time.
There will be time, I will have it so…
For I shall Today Walk Tomorrow Climb a tree!

Going to Hell in a Head Basket, Gregory Anthony Stone, 200

GOING TO HELL IN A HEAD BASKET

No one warned me about building a house on sand and so it was that the angry sea with its sharp fangs swallowed it whole.
"Lucky," most said, "that you were not at home."
No one had taught me what being lucky meant or why some were and some weren't or if that luck, I was never told about, would fluctuate.
Perhaps, it hitches a ride on a bird's wings and when that bird lands and where that bird lands so does luck but merely for a moment or two before it is lifted by the wind and whisked away again.
The where is not important at all now is it?
No one told me about death or the meek inheriting the earth.
We're all Going To Hell In A Head Basket.
I believe they have waited long enough and if they must die before their due inheritance, it is no reward at all.
No one told me about a heaven and a hell.
And, so, I, left to my own theories imagine hell right here, right now.
We're all Going To Hell In A Head Basket.
And heaven, a whimsical fairy tale, is a place, a setting really to entertain or frighten the children of the world into obedience, or to hold the wanderers and questioners in check.
No one prepared me for the reality of all the children who go to bed hungry with roaring bellies
Or the children who die from neglect or abuse so horrific that even I, who have not been prepared, do not understand the why of it all.
We're all Going To Hell In A Head Basket.
No one revealed the truth about majority ruling outcomes and so I listen as those elected to their respective offices make promises

they will not keep and say nothing using a great deal of words.
And I have yet to receive the memo on equality and fairness for they are not the same and in actuality the majority does not rule at all.
That top tier, you know the pyramid used to show the food groups, food the starving children have yet to eat, elude us into believing that what is being done is what we want and what we need.
A new mall, a new amusement park, a new sports arena, another crusade that we know will never really come to fruition for nothing grows on the ground of an ancient ruin engulfed in a miasma whose gaudy mansion cannot be seen even from the greatest of distances.
That distance, that intangible and all too important word that keeps the minority ruling and making all of the decisions that the meek and those on that lower tier, you know, those without food, a home, a career, a job, a future where the gap isn't so wide.
It will not be so.
For We Are All Going to Hell In A Head Basket.
No one told me of such things like the haves and the have not's.
There seem to be more, I think, of those have not's these days and they are too weak from hunger, and a feeling of defeat which may be the only legacy they can leave to their children, to rumble and so there is, sometimes, most times, all the time, no energy to rumble and fight for that equality and fairness.
Kittens, children, on a chain, when we all know there is no need for such shackling.
Oh, there is that cat, that child, that may stray, and we may wonder where it goes and perhaps, yes, perhaps, hope it will find its way to wherever cats go, unleashed.
Keep your cats home, if you have yours still, and watch carefully, very carefully, lest your cat decides to run.
The minority, for a variety of reasons, or none at all, will know, they know. But then again, they've always known.
We don't. We think we do with our opinions and theories and alliances and stoic support to this sector, or another.
It will be fine.

For We Are All Going To Hell In A Head Basket.
You need not concern yourself, or worse still, have it consume you with great fear of being watched, observed, monitored, and ultimately led on that leash that appears tighter than the one before
And should you decide to pick up the pace on your kitten paws, the leash, it is a noose really, will surely strangle the will to fight out of your very soul.
A call to arms of all those young men and women who may or may not return and when or if they do...it is only then that the war, on rediscovering their humanity once again, truly begins.
No one advised me to place my memories, both good and bad, but mostly bad, evil, tragic, even, and horrific, into a container, a pretty box and place it far back into the closet where the cobwebs will eventually cover it all.
A pretty box holding memories that I know I may or may not take down from time to time
I refuse to disturb those cobwebs and find no need to open that pretty box that is not pretty at all
I may choose to bury it.
Or I may choose not to choose at all.
And that is a decision.
And the only decision I need not concern myself with now or ever is that, when the end does come,
We are Going To Hell In A Head Basket.
I did not know I did not know that a moment wasted is a moment lost or that it matters.
And well it should matter after all, and you can choose to agree or disagree or not choose at all.
You see if it matters to you, if it benefits and suits you, or even if it is only in your interest, then your moments will not be wasted and lost.
Not lost, like the cat, that one person, those many people, off its leash away from home ignored, unfed, suffering in agonizing pain from one disease, and there are many, or another, but, you will you not have wasted a second of your life, a second or a fractional part of that second that you will never recoup.
And better still, you will...
I did not know I did not know.

Monsters really do exist sometimes with childlike smiles and innocence but monsters just the same.

They have names, some even more than just one name.

Yes there are monsters; murderers, rapists, pedophiles, sadists, masochists, kidnappers, and all in between.

Some are welcomed in homes where true innocence lives and brutalize the young and old alike. Their fangs come in different shapes and sizes. And all the crusades by this group or that and, yes, there are many have little impact on identifying, acknowledging, or punishing them. Yes, monsters do exist.

And, yes, we are Going To Hell In A Head Basket.

I did not know I did not know.

Stepping on shards of broken glass will most certainly cut into your bare feet, the remnants; fragments really, make their way to your brain where they remain as a reminder to learn from life's lessons.

I did not know I did not know.

That the gashes and cuts, and punctures would heal, but the memory of that day, that moment will not leave you alone. Oh, yes, you could choose to put it away in that pretty cobweb covered box, perhaps, I one day-not yet.

I did not know I did not know.

Most, if not all, snakes hide in wait for their prey. If it is small enough, like a cat, it will strike with its formidable fangs, inject its venom, then, it will swallow you whole.

And so, I have ignored, because I had not been warned about those snakes, I somehow fought the venom that had coursed through my being. It heated my blood, an eruption of lava coursing through each vein, artery, and vessel of my being. Still I lived.

But in the end, I too will be Going To Hell In A Head Basket.

I passed a car the other day. There, all the cats, people really, that had gotten off their leashes or escaped, huddled together in the blustery bitter cold of that January night. There they cuddled warming one against the other.

Meowing in agony, I guessed they had not eaten in days. Their cries echoed in that bitter blustery cold night.

I did not know I did not know.

Many beseech our help for all those starving beings and whether to alleviate our own conscience because all of our cats, our families, are safely home and warm and well-fed, we offer a meager scrap of leftover this or that. And the cynic walks by without a second glance assuming that all those meager scraps or the pittance that is given fills the coffers of the minority, who are also Going to Hell In A Bread Basket when all is done.
Are they truly building mansions and attending extravagant affairs funded by the majority who struggles, often along with his wife, in order to provide for his own family, his cats? And so how much of your conscience really goes to feed those gathered, on this bitter blustery cold night, in the car?
I did not know I did not know.
That when hell and heaven meet, and, I believe, they will, if they have not already, the cats may find it within themselves to meow and claw their way back home. Where the minority does not rule and provide us with distractions that divert our attention from the truth and the majority will gather, no longer entertained and distracted, rise united.
I did not know I did not know.
There is no blame here, for my ignorance is my own, just as yours belongs to you alone. If I am sad, quizzical, skeptical, a conspiracy theorist, a dreamer, an artist, a carpenter, a teacher, an officer, a construction worker, an architect, a cat then let it be so, it will pass. This I know even when there are times and things I did not know I did not know.
I did not know I did not know. Search out your happy; it is there, hiding perhaps momentarily, reach out to it and embrace it. You, I, will know that you, I, will rescue cats, people, the old, the young, and all those in between.
One day, one day, before we will all be Going To Hell In A Bread Basket, be happy!
Despite it all, because of it all
Cats and all...be happy!
And we're All Going to Hell in a Bread Basket...
In a Hand Basket....
In a Head Basket!

All Red

Mass Card, Gregory Anthony Stone, 2013

MASS

Some have congregated seeking atonement, redemption, forgiveness
And so they sit on the hard wooden pews, missile in hand
Reciting the prayers that will lead them to their respective mission
As they listen to the priest reciting the holy message of the day-Redemption
Today he speaks Isaiah 42:7
"To open the blind eyes, to bring out the prisoners from the prison, and them that sit in darkness out of the prison house."
While they stand and cross themselves
While their thoughts take them to their lives beyond those words
Thoughts of work, the meal they will prepare, the children who are no longer home-
Thoughts...it is a mass and as the words filter through the hallowed walls
Some caught in the stained glass windows
Some lingering at the feet of Mary
Those gathered, the mass, try desperately to listen, still in a mission
Seek out atonement, redemption, forgiveness.
A mass.
The congregation at mass that takes them, what they hope, will be the journey to heaven.
A mass and so it is the same yet different like the mass that is found infiltrating
The bodies or brains of old and young alike.
A mass that is sometimes curable and sometimes not-
Like so many homophones, the word will not let me alone
A mass of children playing in the park
And I so yearn to pump my legs that would allow me rise to meet the sky

The park where, in my youth, nothing else mattered
Abandonment, free-spirited, innocent, playful
Where atonement, redemption, forgiveness had yet to find me
Where I park my car and sit and watch what once was-
The same but different like so many
The mass, the park-
And a hook like the priest had tried, desperately, to pass along
It was the word of the Lord
Hoping that his words, the Lord's words, would carry those sitting in those hard
Wooden pews, would take with them closer to heaven as they live day after day.
The hook, the curved metal structure, upon which the live bait is placed-
With the hope that one fish, at least, will take the bait-
The hook held in firm hands, silence, anticipation
The same anticipation found by those trying to hold onto the Word of God.
And so they sit, the reflection of the morning ritual, their pressed clothes, the hair neatly combed-
Groom, the same yet different
The same mass
Where the groom waits anxiously for his bride-to-be.
The mass, where some have left directly after communion
Turning left and exiting through the door
Where some will mouth words to this one or that one exiting after communion,
It is part of their religious rite and so they rise
Leaving directly after some, perhaps making their way to the mouth of the River Jordan
The Dead Sea-
Still, they will search out the Promised Land and so it will be there at the mouth of the
River Jordan where there will be a sharing, a communion of sharing

Taking thoughts and feelings along
The thoughts of the meal they will prepare, the children who are no longer home-
Communion-
The same thoughts and feelings I, sometimes, am willing to share
Feelings that weave in and out of my mind
In a mass of confusion and park themselves there
There where they may be awaiting for some words of comfort
Words, that may carry me, or not, through the week, perhaps-
They will stalk me, unrelenting, challenging me, creating silky black threads
When I so would rather garner stalks of greenery and meander through
Stalks of spider plants and flowers
And gather them all in a large mass of color.
I so do love color!
The reds, blues, greens, yellow, black, and white even though it is not a color at all
I will color the world with the varying hues of all my colors.
A mass array of spurts mingling together
The same but different-
Yes, I shall collect the mass and bring it home to remind me...just to remind me.

With the Father, Gregory Anthony Stone, 2014

WITH THE FATHER

I knew his name as he took me in his arms and hugged me
With welcoming arms and gentle whispers of comfort, love
I did not, would not recoil
What was not familiar, new, loving had found me
And I welcomed it into the core of my weary being.
"Come rest, you have traveled far. Rest," He said.
Where I had been a fish lured by callous hands
And taken to the shore
And gasped what I thought would be my final breath
Floundering back and forth, writhing in pain
Up then down seeking what had been my home
Hoping that somehow I would get there before death came…
But the pure and innocent hands of a child,
And while I had questioned and even doubted all
Those pure and innocent hands
Lifted me and cast me back into the water
Where I took in the impurities and chaos of the world
Filtered them out and drew in life.
"Welcome home. Welcome home."
It was here that the colors came alive
All the colors I had seen and ignored.
Colors coming together…alive, bright
Overtaking me
And, comforted, loved me with a lightness of both heart and mind.
I was home.

Lost Soul, Gregory Anthony Stone, 2014

LOST SOUL

I am a solitary wolf standing on a precipice
Howling at the moon...sad...grieving, lost
Will no one listen to my cry?
As I ponder, far away from my pack, plummeting into the abyss
My paws, my feet, my arms caught in the wind
And even that will not affect the impact
Not today...not today
When all is grey
And my only friend right now is my bed.
Curled in an enormous sadness
That, at present, only my bed, my friend, can understand.
Where the only visible sign of life is the rise and fall of my breast!
The lost and lonely canvas nestled up against the wall
Awaits my return, its white sorrowful glare reminds of my own
Sorrow.
And I realize, know, that even with my pack far in the distance
I do not travel alone.
You see, there are many wolves that wish to free fall into the grey
abyss
And like me, they do.
So great is our sadness.
Where thoughts define
Unite
Though, on some days, I wish it were not so.
Still, they cling and speak to mind, my thoughts
Of loss and grief and even sorrow
A world where I am not a solitary wolf
Standing on that precipice where all I see is not grey
I peer down long I know you, I know you!
It is my lost and lonely canvas
Awaiting my return.
But my thoughts, my demons, still dictate my every move.

They haunt me with their constant angry screams
Where every involuntary move, and even the voluntary ones
Hurt my being, my body, my arms, my legs, my head where the things I feel
Fill me with sadness, sorrow, loss and creation becomes that grey haze.
And the rise and fall of my the breath comes and reminds me, that I am alive
Not living, just alive.
Paralyzed without inspiration, the grieving brush, clean and ready, clutched firmly in my hand
I know it wishes to leave and needs so desperately to reaffirm its friendship with
The lonely canvas.
They wish to become one with my soul...
Where each moment meets an hour, then a day
Followed by many more
Until the colorful soul explodes onto the canvas
That is all there is...That is who I am
Just not today, not today...
Soon!

The Dove Has Flow, Gregory Anthony Stone, 200

THE DOVE HAS FLOWN

PART I

It was the 60's
Afros, the bigger the better
Balsa Wood Airplanes better than...
Paper ones-
Until the kids that the glue
Would provide a higher flight.
Banana Seats
Long and curved at the back
What a ride!
Barbie dolls...
Rabid Beatles and mania-together.
Bellbottoms, Black Light-
A purple haze...
(Didn't help me much)
Bellbottoms, Bouffant Hairdo
Time consuming and many tools...
All wanting, wishing to resemble Jackie Kennedy...
It soon would end...John's gone...it would end.
Bomb proof Fallout shelters-
Providing the illusion that somehow they would
Keep one safe should Cuba decide to launch
Its bombs.
Children rushed and huddled-practicing-just in case
Their heads touching their knees as they sat
Quietly waiting for the impact
That thankfully never came!
But shelters built
Some with the bare essentials
Whatever they might be-
Some, like small guesthouses, equipped with pool tables,

Paintings and wine cellars…
Go-Go boots, Nancy Sinatra-
Granny glasses-John Lennon, Roger McGuinn
Like Benjamin Franklin
And soon died out-
No longer cool.
Hair Ironing and Lava Lamps
Illuminated colorful glass cylinder
Wax for heat-
The 60's-
Miniskirts, go-go boots,
the Dove Has Flown.
Colorflower stickers on automobiles, walls, windows, waste
Baskets- Rickie Tickie Stickers.
Bottle caps thrown within the
Boundaries of chalked white lines
Scully-
Sea monkeys and Slogan Buttons-McKinley and Bryan
And hippie backpacks
A voice, sentiments, declarations, and politics…
Slot cars, Superballs-
Made of Zectron-synthetic
Infiltrating the White House…
Smiley Faces!
Gidget is surfing while Chubby Checkers is…
Doing the Twist!

Tie Dye T-shirts...
A rainbow explosion of swirling colors-designs
Ancient Art and self-expression-
Troll dolls-they will bring you luck
Green hair, red, purple, yellow...
Luck as you make way to your Fallout Shelter
Just in case!
Catch it quickly, if you can, in the dark, deep
Of the green forest.
Beatniks, flower children, Johnny Carson, Sammy Davis Jr., Senator Robert Kennedy, Paul Newman and Steve McQueen in Turtlenecks!
Perhaps, to cover their heads and make
Retreat in their private
Fallout Shelter-
Woodstock, War, Protests, Peace
Free Love, Marijuana, Brownies, and Chocolate Chip Cookies...
the Dove has Flown!

PART II

Rebellions, connections, a call to action...
It was the 60's...
When the call of artists, musicians, writers, and poets
Screamed out the melancholy
State of the world
Some would be heard
While others ignored...
I carried them all with me well into the 70's-
Bob Dylan, Sylvia Plath, Allen Ginsberg, Lawrence Ferlingetti, Gary Snyder, Nikki Giovanni, May Swenson, Seamus Heaney
Countee Cullen, Claude McKay, Jean Toomer. Langston Hughes
Initiating rebirth
A Renaissance-
Later, I realized
the Dove has Flown.

PART III

I kissed your lemon-honey flavored lips
My tongue circling your tongue
My body aching with the feel of you-
And you welcomed me.
I covered your face with kisses
Of innocence
Free love.
My love beads some matching the color of your eyes
Professed my love
As if there was any need
Any need at all!
And you wore them affectionately
Fingering them from time to time-
Perhaps, as a reminder of our love
Perhaps, counting the days, the years
We'd spend together
And we shared the Mood Ring
Though there was no need then-
We were one, after all.
Each step bringing us closer
Then, slowly, so slowly
My body ached less-
And the lemon-honey lips
Left for weeks on end
Taunted me as you lay your beads
Aside-
I never did find them again
the Dove Has Flown
High above the summer skies
Where rainbows appear after a torrential rain...
We would not let it be
And so we ignored the caressing of colors
That managed, somehow, to keep their identity intact.
And the Mood Ring we had shared, that I held onto till...
No longer-

You garnered one of your own.
And my mind, though the words never reached my lips-
Fuck you!
Leave me the Fuck Alone!
But you knew, you knew...
Though the words never reached my lips...
the Dove Has Flown
In flight, it took the innocence of first love
And replaced it... ritual or lust
And, I found, they were one and the same
Retracing my footsteps along the muddy waters
Along the swamp, searching out the weeping willow
I found solitude.
It was there that my footsteps alighted
Leaving reminders that still exist
And it was there where I sought out the words
Of all the poets of the Renaissance
For I, too, was awaiting, initiating a rebirth
That would not come as it had in Harlem.
And with final guttural scream
It found its way to my lips-
Get the fuck out!
You did. I did.
And in so doing, I took my love beads,
My Mood Ring and the memory of footsteps
Which are still there along the muddy swamp
Where the Weeping Willow calls it, "home"-
And I've no need of a Fallout Shelter
Though the bomb has fallen
And left neither of us surviving
In the aftermath, but for memories
And could have beens
Should have beens

What we assumed, in our innocence, knew
Would be our future
Love Beads and Mood Rings
But, it is there, in the cool breeze, where I can finally see
Accept
the Dove has flown!

Portrait in Darkness, Gregory Anthony Stone, 2

HUMANITY YOU SAY?

Sitting on the threshold of something
Waiting for nothing that always comes
And there it sinks to the depths
Of what we call humanity
Tearing at its heart, ravaging it to shreds and tatters.
Why does it not die a tumultuous death…peace
As it sinks to the murky waters of an unforgiving, angry sea?
No, it will not be.
It floats there on the cusp of a fog-laden rainbow
Glistening, shining, restored with hope of its making
Pumping anew a life restored.
Humanity You Say?
A breath whispering on the spring wind
Live, rejoice, find yourself arisen within
The miasma of a stagnant humanity
Whose imputes, its lethargy has been
Lying in wait for such a moment.
Such is the soul that sits on the threshold of enmity.
Humanity You Say?
Infants, innocent, unaffected by the temptations
Yet to come.
Youth unflustered in the search for balance-
Fall stoic in the need for prudence
In a world where conditions exist
Such that the winter never comes to grace the earth with white
Standing
Sitting
Tattered hearts that crack then mend, perhaps
A formidable gap created, destroyed
Only to be rebuilt again over and over again.

They are dying not dead
Living not alive
And they echo from within and those
Who choose to listen...
Humanity You Say?
Such is the essence of the chaff that within it
Lies the rebirth of the world...
Humanity You Say?

Sissy, Gregory Anthony Stone, 2014

(WOMAN)

To woman dying young
There may be rest
A respite.
Found in the breath of a whisper on
The wind to grieve
Her beauty…soul.
Mayhem…sadness of
A catacomb
There lies her life.
Do you not see it?
And in the echo of the raindrop…
In the distance
Come more and more.
She weeps
Upon earth's bosom
And it welcomes her grief
And holds it tenderly.
To live for loss
And she finds it
Resonating with hollow reminders
Let go.
While the woodpecker refuses
To peck on a dying limb
Let it go
You are woman, after all.
Until the echo
Dies on the fallen limbs
Of the long ago..
To a woman dying young
The echo follows her
And she covers her ears
From the pain of it all.

The Horse's Ass, Gregory Anthony Stone, 2011

RETURN

Waiting endlessly for the return of spring
And the cherry blossoms that fill
The meadows
Their sweet, sweet smell
Intoxicating Life!
Pink, white buds swaying
Keeping rhythm
At sun rise.
And in the breeze that come
We wait sitting...
Hoping for what we see again.
Cherry blossoms in the wind.

Camouflage, Gregory Anthony Stone, 2013

THE OLIVE BRANCH

We let our minds
Revel and even welcome the heaviness of it
All!
The singleness of the Olive Branch
Is solitary
In the heavy winter's snow.
How can this be?
And we close our eyes to the murderer
Who cuts the yellow heart
That bleeds out in stone.
The stilled talons of the muddied
Dove
Felled in flight
And its muted coo reveals
Through black beads
Now hollowed out
Siphoned
Lies bearing the Olive Branch.

Packaging Lapel GAS Rolling Papers, Gregory Anthony Stone,

THE WELCOMING

I held it on my tongue
Like papyrus stuck
To the roof of my mouth
It withdrew, dissolved
To the cavern
Of my anticipating, waiting soul
Where the light would guide its path.
And there it lay, still melting
Clinging, fusing to nothing and all.
Silently, it cleansed in a ritual
Of blood and a feast
Famine.

Don't Think, Just Feel, Gregory Anthony Stone, 1968

WAKE

Next to the shell
Lying within a silk covered box
I sit staring at the caked
Mask of death.
It is not me
Here and nowhere
Everywhere.
Beside the a shell sealed shut
The eyes, the lips, the bones re-shaped,
Broken, cut
Formaldehyde and I
Watching
With a passing tear-
The dry dew upon the withered flowers.
Who are you?
And at a distance
I carried and discarded
Memories
As you come to watch me
Still.
Laughing, the warmth of the light in you
All too quickly gone
Frozen, frigid
Do you ignore the buzzing of the fly?
I swatted it for you
And it landed flat
Upon your tissue filled chest
And your mouth, sealed shut
You did not protest.
You share your death
Your fingers crossed
Well-manicured
Motionless with their hue of pink
It does not suit you well
It does not suit you well

Beckoning Still, Gregory Anthony Stone, 1968

COME QUICKLY OR NOT AT ALL

Nebulous-a mist, vapors, scanned, released
Dare I, should I, will I?
But my idle mind, my stilled hands, my feet
Stop
Afraid to touch-
Fear, inertia, complacency, lethargy
Weave black spider threads
And I fall short of my destination.
Afraid the venomous spider will awake
And in my old worn shoes
That fit me well
(I am not willing, ready to let them go)
Cover my horny toes
That protrude
From time to time
And the laces long since gone
The soles that once held the leather in check
Hunger to be fed
Their tongues, a reminder, like the lapping dog
Licking an empty water bowl-
And so I walk more slowly, cautiously
Without destination
Possibilities
Expectations
Results
Action
Decisions
Not today, not today!
And the will within me begs
How?
It is good to feel
But, decided not to decide
Giving way to my worn old shoes
That still fit me well!

Hungry Cat, Gregory Anthony Stone, 1996

CLUTTERED WALLS

Divinity, fate
Barred the sparrow
From taking of the earth
Famine.
And it looks to empty hands-
Sitting on the dry fountain
That once quenched its
Dry throat.
It makes no sound
And so they wait
For a prophet that never comes
While the worms
Lay buried beneath
Unaffected, uncaring
Burrowing deeper to the recesses
Of wherever their
Moist, dirt covered skin
May lead.
And the sparrow waits
For the feast of maggots to start
Anew
And an Eternity to death!

Healing the Lepers, Gregory Anthony Stone, 1978

FOR ONE

He sits alone on a rickety
Bar room stool
Carefully balancing it on
Its two hind legs
And it creaks and moans
Beneath him-
His weight more than any could bear.
And his large, dirt covered hands
Tap away the passing of his...life
Moments All!
His lips tight against the toothpick
That he maneuvers back and forth
By his snake like tongue
Between decay and rot
Back and forth
A pendulum on his mother's
Heirloom clock.
And his soiled and moth eaten shirt
The one he has worn each and every day
For as long as he can remember
Reveals his soul.
And he shakes
The stool giving way
As he crumbles to the sawdust covered
Floor
Like his dreams crushed by his own weight.
One more beer, more pretzels
Between a burp and a sleepy
Yawn
While his fingers tap
Tap his life away.

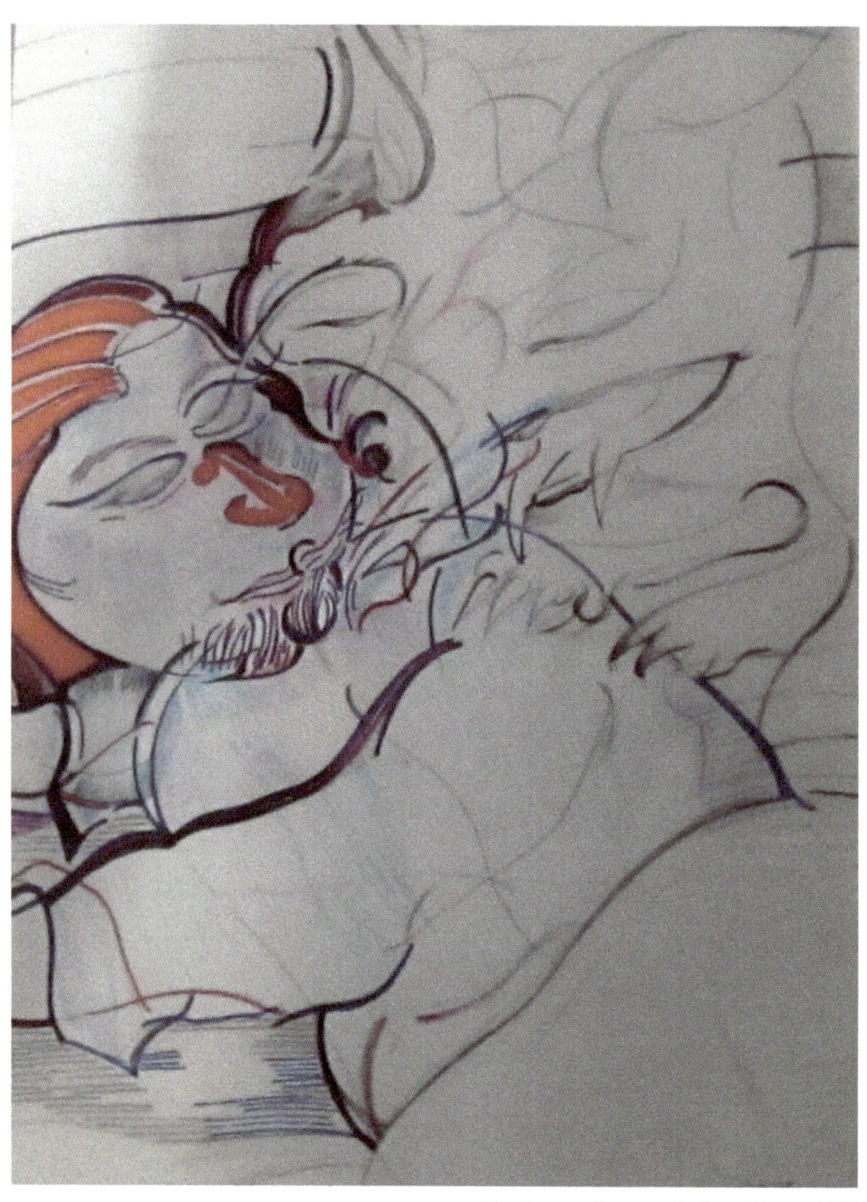

The Dream, Gregory Anthony Stone, 1998

EVENING COMES ANEW

A vesper in the night
Dies
No one is listening, after all!
It falls heavily
Upon the windowsill
Of the world
Where no one listens
And is whisked away with the dust and dirt
Of a tattered shirt that
Smells of dry paint and turpentine.
In death, muted, unheard
(For no one ever listens)
Falls upon the cold hard
December soil
Frozen, frigid, crushed, cursed, ridiculed
Blends and does not rise
But still manages to whisper
Through the jasmine in the night-
Just listen.

Sorrow, Gregory Anthony Stone, 201.

NOT

Curl up into a ball
In a vat of scalding water
Muffle the sobs
That you hear outside
And come out stillborn.
The eternal infant-
Flushed out in a cesspool with the bile
Of the dead.
Sever life with the sharp edge of my tongue
And let the crimson ooze
Out into the world
That will cover the world with the flaming of
My sunset.
The tomahawk in skeleton fingers
Too brittle to hold on.
And the fossil embedded in ancient rocks
Reveal a time passing
And if I no longer see the moon
On whose smiling face
Rests eternity
Then I could...if I wanted to
If I wanted to.

False Prophet, Gregory Anthony Stone, 2013

AND WHEN

The white smooth fur of a rabbit's foot
Dried and hanging lifeless
On the chain
In the grasp of sweaty palms.
While the other hand
Trembles at the undone
Button-hole
Of an unlaced tie up boot
Stiff...it cracks
Falling in pieces onto the floor.
And the hands on the clock
Record the passing of time
Soon stilled
The battery
Rusted
Acid leaking
In its plastic casing
Is replaced and cleaned
And replaced upon the wall
No one ever paints.
A house on fire
A house on fire...
The rabbit foot in hand
Once white
Innocent
Is masked by gray haze
Of a House on Fire!

Under the Spell, Gregory Anthony Stone, 2012

AUTONOMY

Diseased with sores uncleansed
It wreaked with the stench of death,
While its black tentacles
Reach down and grasp
Hold on
Own you!
And there the festering sore
Unhealed-
Clouded black
And liquefied
A mixture of acid and rot
It is a Beginning
And an End...
Is it?

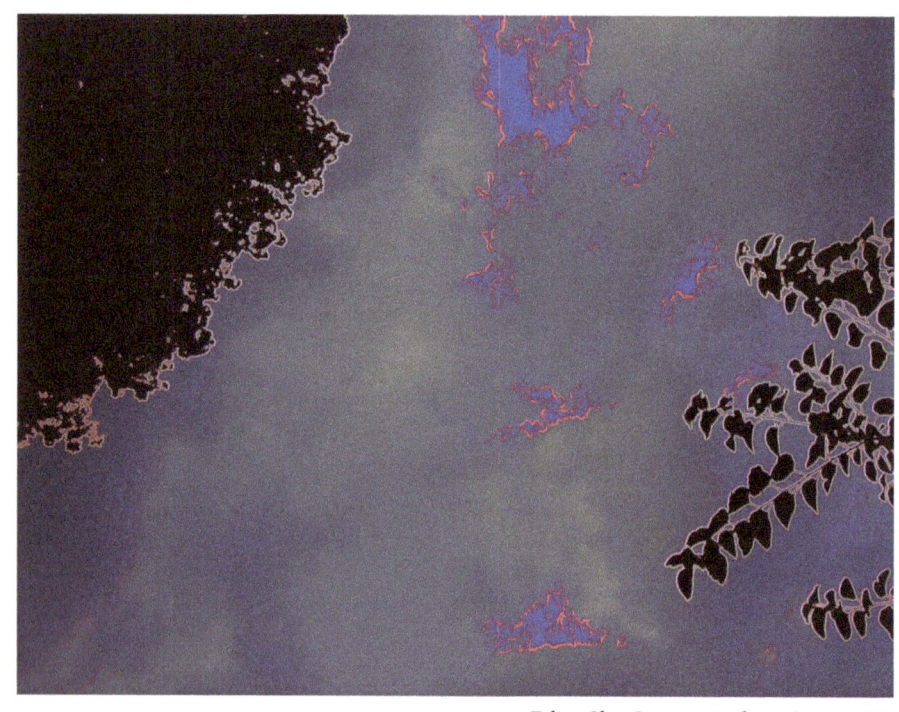

Feline Sky, Gregory Anthony Stone, 2013

ORGASM

Hold me gently in your arms of steel
And smother me with your warm kisses
Hold my hand if you so choose
Or caress my auburn hair
You need not penetrate
To take me to my climax
I am alive in the comfort
Of your being.
Do not whisper
Banal words of this or that
Meaningless, void of emotion
Love
I know the difference.
Comfort me
With that familiar
Empathy I've come to cherish...
My moans will follow
And I shall call your name
In whispers and ecstasy
Then I shall know
You have given me your all!
Cover me with kisses
That will allow my lids to close
So that the beast of the world
Makes a hasty retreat
Into oblivion.
Then I shall find
The greater heights-
My climax...and it will be yours
I shall be yours!
Share your dreams and I
Shall lend you mine-

Allow me to melt into your heart
Fill your mind with madness
Embrace your soul
Landing my warm mouth
Upon yours where we shall be one-
Spoon feed me-I shall not resist
Let it be the truth
Then I shall reach that height
I shall moan...I shall call your name
Over and over again
I shall moan...I shall call your name.
Hold me gently in your arms of steel
Your strength, my strength...we shall find as one.
Be my lover...my first-
My last...
I shall reach greater heights
My climax...
An orgasm of love, tender words, comfort
Safety, loyalty
Void of meaningless words
That bring to question
Intimacy...or lust?
Let it not be a ritual...
There is no climax to be found there-
Come alight on my breast
As you hold onto me
And take me...
With your words
Your dreams
Your comfort
Orgasm!

Who Is The Masked Man, Gregory Anthony Stone, 1976

MARMALADE AND TOAST

Orange marmalade and toast
I cannot pick the rinds
Out
Poe is
Dead
The fissure deflected by the pool
Ripples of Pallas
By stone
Circle, circle
The ending.
And the beginning of Caesura
I cannot serve
The Prince
Orange marmalade and toast.

Crazy Commuter, Gregory Anthony Stone, 201

ROAD

Large letters etched
Yellow   NOPARKING
On a crowded city street.

Empty glass bottles the labels
Lost
The soiled tissue
Crumbled
At the curb-
A dirty brown paper bag
A worn out black shoe
Left-over food of this or that
A tattered red and brown shirt
Its owner nowhere to be found
A woman sitting
Her back hunched over
With the cares of years gone
Too quickly by
Her matted, unwashed hair
Under the ill-fitting wool hat
The coat she wears
Too small to cover her shivering body
In the snow that now is covered
With a large smattering of greys and black
From the fumes of too many cars
And trucks.
She sits…she waits…
Looking upon the empty wrapper
A passing crave
Now gone.
Disorganized, organized clutter
In the rain and ice that
Will not erase the painted yellow.

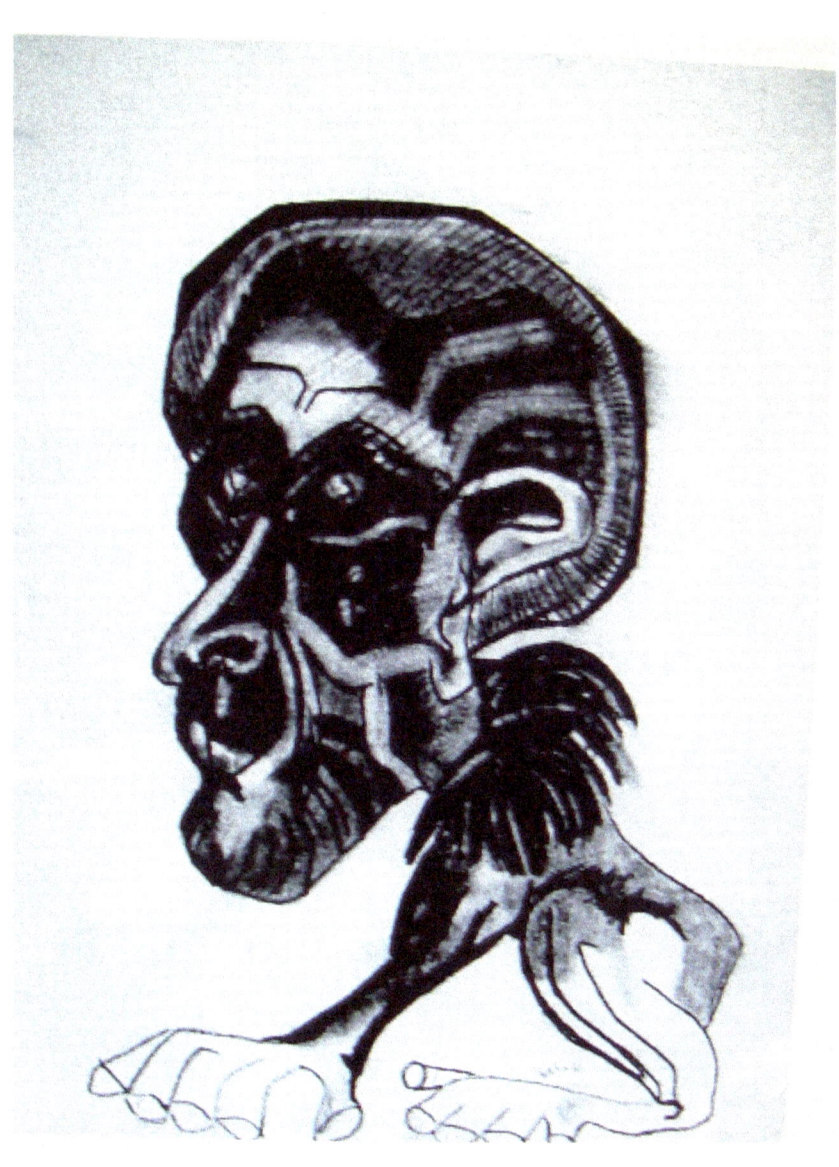

Lion, Gregory Anthony Stone, 1968

EVIL IS SANE

Rubbish
Mutilated
One-hundred seventy times
Over
Strategically hidden in the black
Garbage bag
Behind, underneath, alongside the road
Beneath the highway
Decaying, dying over and over...
Do not be fooled...
When do beings find
Insanity likened to evil?
License to kill
When does sanity become evil?
Humanness?
The brain, your mind, your energy,
Mass confusion?
Sanity out of place
Evil
A life
None.

Maryann Decaying, Gregory Anthony Stone, 2010

ANCIENT

Daffodils...
Sweet spring carries me
Remember?
The decaying stones
An ancient fort
A convent
A monastery
A winery?
Harboring still-the sweet smell of spring
And the thicket on the path does not
Cover the stones...
Forgot
Stumbled
Hit my sorrow against the weeds
Died instantly
And there daffodils grew.

Frustration, Gregory Anthony Stone, 1971

BE

Cease the flutter of its wings
And it will no longer fly
Against the window
Pain of the world
Watch it fall upon the white
Ledge
Hitting it again and again
Finally
Grey matter oozes
Out
Against
The Black
Emptiness...
Death
Against a hazy sky.

The Decision, Gregory Anthony Stone, 1970

COLLECTIONS

Gathered memories
Confined in the rusty old tin can
The memories of youth
We remember only to forget
When the fetus plug's undone
A voyage taken
Realized
And the sunken ship in Atlantis
A mermaid at its helm
You seek a tunnel where none
Exists to the ocean
Gathered memories
And a smoky stair two flights
Up
To...

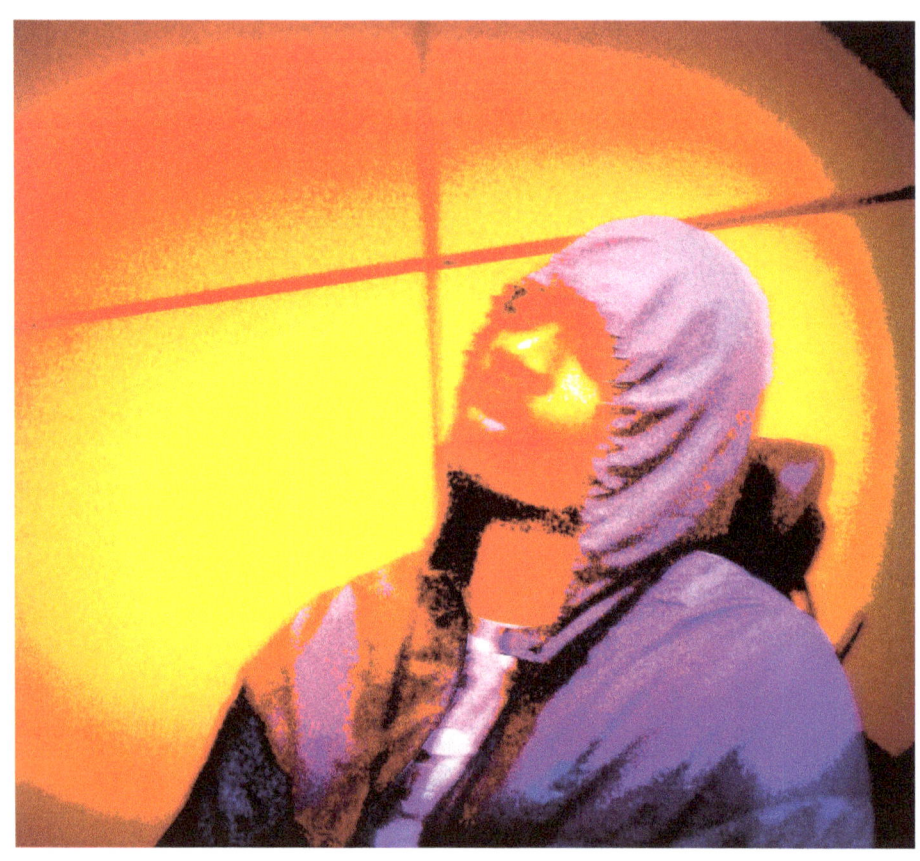

Mack in the Blood Red Aura, Gregory Anthony Stone, 2012

LOOK BUT DO NOT SEE

The shadow of the Earth from the distance
Reveals the charcoal that does not burn
And so you disagree...
You have proven otherwise
it makes no difference
To me.
Charcoal does not burn
Your eyes, long ago, gouged out
Replaced with opaque marbles
(and not the ones of many colors or swirling patterns)
You pranced around the truth
You were, after all, born of the Steppes
On a blue velvet, like royalty you were told
Beyond the plain...or plane
Out of reach
Unaffected
Blind
But, charcoal, truly does not burn
Alone!

No 2 Face Here, Gregory Anthony Stone, 2013

ONCE

Friends
Prosperity
Adversity
Fear
Fresh tears
Disappointed
Pretense
Closure
A sad song
Break....
Remember
Loyalty
Smiling
Laughter
Sunshine
Strength
Acceptance
You!

In Another Light, Gregory Anthony Stone, 2013

JUSTICE AND JUST ICE
PART I

I passed the small light gray and pink cape house
My children at my side making our way to school.
"Look, mom," my son said, "there it is again!"
An old worn stick held the sign
The one that seemed to scream out at us
Each and every day.
Affixed to that stick
The faded brown cardboard announced a statement
Dog Stool had been written upon it
An arrow directly beneath it-
Directing your gaze where it
Had been left.
Each day, without fail, the sign
Was moved from one place to another
Just outside the perimeter of a white
Three wooden barred fence.
And, it was on one warm early spring day
When justice found me!
There she knelt tending to the marigolds
That she had planted
As was her habit each and every spring
This much I knew, had seen.
"Good Morning," I said.
"Yes, it is," was her reply.
And so it went each and every day-
The woman who lovingly tended her marigolds
Donning a purple straw hat
And the Dog Stool sign moved once again
The same sign that spawned
Jeers, jokes, and nightmarish stories
By the neighborhood children-

She didn't own a car-
And as far as I could tell,
She had no visitors
Except for the weekly delivery boys
From the local supermarket or
The pharmacy.
Though, on occasion, I had seen her
Get out of a cab and make her way,
Slowly and with careful steps, back into her
Light gray and pink house.
I didn't hear the echo of a bell
Nor footsteps that would surely follow
And allow me entrance
If she so chose.
I knocked, waited, knocked again.
I heard the unlatching of a bolt
The turning of the doorknob
And the door slowly opened.
There she stood, the one the neighborhood
Children feared as Hanzel and Gretel
Feared the witch that caught and
Caged them up
Later to be eaten.
I had no such fears
As I held my basket of freshly baked
Blueberry muffins in one hand
And a small box of chocolates
In the other.
"Good Morning," I said.
"Yes, it is." She replied as the sun cascaded past me
And fell on her not so long ago gone
Youth.
"Come in, come in."
I hadn't expected that welcome
Not in the least.
"I'll make some tea."
And as I entered her quaint cape,

I noticed, there, upon a credenza
Her purple hat sitting upon the resin head of
A mannequin whose torso,
Its limbs were long since gone.
The purple straw hat she wore as she planted marigolds,
The purple, the same hue of the sashes
Which hang over the garage doors
Of this Hook and Ladder Company
Are another
Announcing the death of a fallen firefighter
Black and purple together yet separate.
They mark a death, a passing.
She poured the water over the tea bag
"It's lemon and honey flavored-bitter and sweet.
You can add more honey if you wish."
I did as the aroma of apples and cinnamon
Found me.
She sat and undid the plastic wrap
That surrounded the box of chocolates
Lifted the lid revealing the selection.
"Please, take one." She offered.
I hesitated-they were for her.
I did without searching out my favorite.
"I so love chocolate…"
We sat in a comfortable silence for a while
"My daughter would have been just about your age."
It took me by surprise
As I nibbled on my chocolate.
"Her name was Victoria and her hair was dark auburn
Just like yours."
"Victoria,' I repeated.
Then it came-
A smile, so much unlike the Mona Lisa…
(Who some have concluded that she had many secrets-intriguing
secrets…
All her own).
But, her smile, as she finished the last of her chocolate

And reached for the freshly baked blueberry muffin,
Was caught somewhere between knowing
And accepting.
"Victoria." She repeated.
"Yesterday," she continued, "or so it seems-
I had been invited to an event
I haven't attended any since."
I didn't question, I sat in the now
And sipped my tea
As she stopped now and then
That smile, the one somewhere between
Knowing and accepting, would cross her face.
"Children fear me. Many fear what they do not or-
Understand. It's how it should be, especially, for children."
"But some children can be so cruel. And I can understand your reason
For placing the sign out on your lawn.
It is not so with children."
"It serves as a reminder, not just for them,
But for me as well."
I watched her face, her eyes, and turned my head
Slightly, to look upon the hat once more
That sat atop the well-worn face of the
Plastic eyes that had no eyes, no lips.
"My husband died many years ago
Fighting for justice only to find
Just Ice…and so it is…and so is life."
And I listened no longer taking tiny bites of the
Blueberry muffin I had taken from my basket.
"I watched as they strapped him to the bed-
More like a gurney really
Attached him to an IV and slowly injected
Him with a sedative first-
Death would follow.
Justice for my Victoria," she said.
My mind reeled as she shared and continued
To share.

"It seems like yesterday."
And there it was again,
That smile somewhere between knowing and
Accepting.
"She was stripped of her innocence...
And, unlike the children who fear what they
Do not know or understand,
She followed him
(Though I know not why)
He took her then,
Her innocence and with a tightening grip
Took her breath along with it.
So I sat, along with others, justice
But the blood within my veins
Became cold and colder still...
Just Ice...
Where is the justice...I shall not
Watch her as she prepares for her senior prom
More than likely, wearing a purple gown,
It was her favorite color, after all.
Perhaps, she would marry and bear my
Grandchildren and together we would
Talk, drink tea, and eat chocolate as the children
Played in my, now, vacant room...
That, too, is now cold and filled with Just Ice."
"I..." dumbfounded and confused realized the memory
Behind the smile somewhere between knowing and accepting.
"Yes, there is no name for a mother who loses a child...
Such pain has no name...no justice can be found there,
After all...and the pain and agony
Of those dying young is not justice after all.
And yes, I plant my marigolds
My purple hat, that provides some comfort,
Reminds me of the difference...and it does exist
Between Justice and Just Ice
And my sign, Dog Stool with its arrow that points
To the place that should be free thus allowing

The grass to grow green and full-
Goes ignored, no one comes back to clean it up-
Perhaps, they too know that shit smells worse
When it lays there for days and once stirred
Smells worse than when it was first
Released by a guided dog.
Or, perhaps, the owner knows and needs reminders
That, sometimes the world is a cesspool
Of evil where Justice is not Justice after all-
"Just Ice."
She offered me another chocolate which I took
And together we sat in a comfortable silence.

PART II

I stopped at the sliding glass doors
Affixed the badge to my blouse
And entered the Veteran's Hospital
As I would do on a bi-weekly basis.
The clerk greeted me as he did each time I visited
And I moved on past him
And made my way toward the rooms
Where healing soldiers waited.
I knocked on the first open door
I came to and was invited in.
"Good morning," I said.
"Yes, it is." He replied.
I approached his bedside with my basket
Of freshly baked blueberry muffins
And box of chocolates.
It was a face I had not seen before-
And he greeted me with a smile
Between knowing and accepting.
"My name is Victor," he said.
Was he?
"Chocolates," he continued as I handed him the box.
"I love chocolate," he said and proceeded to undo
The plastic wrapping and open the lid.
He offered me one first
Which I hesitantly accepted.
I placed my basket on the nightstand
Next to his bed where a fuzzy
Black stuffed bear sat.
"I called him Boots not long ago," he offered as he noticed the
Direction of my gaze.
I smiled.
"My mother brought him to me

Shortly after I arrived-
She took him off my bed at home. He was my childhood friend
And kept the monsters away." He said as he smiled again.
"I've renamed him now. I call him Justin."
"Justin?" I asked.
"Yes. It suits him better. Come sit and we'll talk a while."
I did.
"Justin, how about a story for our visitor?" he said as he reached
over with his right hand
(His left arm had no hand and his legs, I realized were gone as
well)
And took hold of Justin and cradled him to his chest.
"Fighting a war seeking out Justice," he began,
"For people, who need protection, liberty, and the freedom to
choose.
"Yes, I chose to fight for Justice. And fate or a calling to get there
Just In time...
I ignored the warnings of the perils that lay hidden, buried be-
neath the sands
And fields. Just in time to step on a landmine
Shrapnel finding its way to my legs, my arms, my face...and I ques-
tioned
Justice...and a resounding voice screamed
"Just Ice!"
It was then, I noticed that the bear
Was wearing a medal pinned to its chest-
A purple heart
Shiny purple cloth surrounded its perimeter
Colored in gold.
George Washington dead center-
Purple as the background...
Surrounded by the heart.
The president, all presidents, at least after
1917
Gave the soldiers who had been wounded or had died
In battle-
(As if they or the family, some left behind, needed reminding)

Again, the smile somewhere between knowing and accepting
As we sat in a comfortable silence.
He asked for a freshly baked blueberry muffin
The chocolate since gone
"Sorry, we don't have any tea," he said and smiled. "There's no justice."
Again the smile somewhere between knowing and accepting,
He added, "Needless to say, I won't be wearing Boots any time soon."
Had it been any other time, it would have been
Quite funny, and I might have even laughed.
I didn't.
And as I left his room and continued on to several
Rooms where soldiers were healing
From their visible scars, and some healing from
Invisible ones and whose minds had succumbed
Just Ice, I thought-
As they, I knew, were reliving the horrors of fighting for
Justice.
I walked down the hall
Victor's parting words following me
"Just in in time to watch the birth of my first son," he said proudly.
Justice.

PART III

I had never stopped in the chapel before-
I did just then
If only to sit for a while the many
Thoughts ran through my mind-
I opened the solid wood door
And entered.
I elected to sit in one of the back pews
Deep in thought
Perhaps, justice or, at the very least, the hope for justice
Would find me.
I hadn't heard the door open
Nor had I heard any footsteps.
She sat within inches of me
And I noticed, before anything else,
The smile that came from somewhere between knowing and accepting.
And we sat in a comfortable silence
Looking to the altar behind which a large cross
Had been anchored…
Just Ice…Just Ice…just kept repeating itself
Over and over again in my mind
Justin time, the comfortable silence was broken
I welcomed it.
"Humanity cannot exist in world filled with Just Ice." She said.
And I looked into her eyes,
Finding something familiar and comforting
There.
I noticed her auburn hair cascading down her back
And I didn't question why she was wearing a gown
It was early evening after all
Perhaps, she stopped to visit someone
Before attending an event or other.

It was beautiful-
Purple lace with a satin black sash surrounding her waist
Her neck covered with the same purple lace
Upon which clear crystals emitted
Soft rays in the dim lights of the chapel.
"Have you finished your visit?" I asked.
Her smile was her only reply as I continued.
"I hope they're doing well."
"They'll mend. I have no doubt about them mending." She said.
"One can hope...we can only hope."
"Hope, yes, hope where Justice replaces Just Ice and where the cesspool
Created by the uncaring who will not add or stir up the old remnants of their dogs."
A dry, wry, smile crossed my face-
I knew I heard those similar words once before
But, wrapped in my melancholy state
I ignored them.
"You can turn away, but, you already know that it is when
Someone appears that they don't need you at all,
That they need you the most."
"Your fear of the witch consuming you has long since gone-
"But through your innocence, which remains with you still,
Your doubts will fade-
And so that comfortable silence greeted us once again-
I said nothing, neither did she
She reached out and caressed my hand
Smiled the smile that came from somewhere between
Knowing and accepting.
We sat for a while-
Until finally, her hand lifted and placed it
Into the other...
I looked again upon the cross behind the altar
And neither feeling nor sensing her retreat,
She was gone.
I looked down upon the pew where she had sat
Just inches away

Moments ago
And in the dimness of the chapel
Picked up the box she had left behind-
A box of chocolates-
Upon which two solitary words
Etched in gold upon that purple box
Found me...
Justice...Victoria!

In Search of Mr. Hyde, Gregory Anthony Stone, 1998

WHEN I DIE

When I die, I shall not lament the golden road outstretched
To its own will.
I shall not pine the hunger for
Unsatisfied passion.

I shall not hold in judgment those seeking only
My survival
When
I yearned and sought
To live.

I shall not stand unwelcoming at the foot
Of the altar.

Like all those before me
Who know not where I loved.

I shall not yearn another second
In the existence
Of that translucent
Solitude.
Alone, I shall not go forth-back and up
Again.

I shall not question the moment that will
Follow
All those that came before-

I shall not hollow out my heart
Replace it with black cotton clouds of doubt
This I shall know-
And in the knowing
Will be my existence
Still.

Yellow Snow, Gregory Anthony Stone, 2010

DIS COVERED

Is there a place on earth that has yet to be discovered?
While the boisterous politicians with their many words that address nothing
Have us all convinced that the economic solution is now discovered...
Yes, some of us say, we have been this covered in rising numbers on the non-existing statistics of those not collecting unemployment
Yet, they assure us that unemployment is on its downswing...
And I'm not grateful about being this covered...
I can search my way through reality and see some living in their "I can't buy gas because of the rising costs and I'm one of those who is not employed" and not in your statistics
I am not the only one who is this covered
And I am tired of being this covered by nonsense words and unfilled promises that will keep my hungry children hungry and living on the edge of being
This covered!
Our home, that was mortgaged and re-mortgaged, now sits, with its eyes shut to the fact that the banks have made it theirs so that we can live in our gas-empty car...
My home has also been this covered by greedy banks and corrupt executives waving their private victory flags of discovery...they needn't pay attention to those left this covered.
And while assurances come about the shaky ground of Social Security Benefits, I wonder if anyone has checked in with the elderly who long ago were this covered?
We talk about peace and then talk some more,
Bring home our troops, some whole (or are they), some wounded, some not at all...

Has anyone told them they had been or will be this covered? Thus, some yearn for the voyages to end and begin a new journey where there may be no reason to find a need to discover a way out…

Because some of us know that being this covered spawns a new breed, perhaps a dying breed, of those who were once believers, followers, voyagers ever hopeful of finally reaching solid ground…

Yes, I have been this covered…and owe more than I can pay, eat less than my body needs, cry in the night from the cold that creeps in through the shattered window of our gasless car, skip a dose of pills here and there, just to make them last a bit longer, listen for the pounding to begin hinting the running of the bulls…

But I grieve, wishing I were not discovered at all!

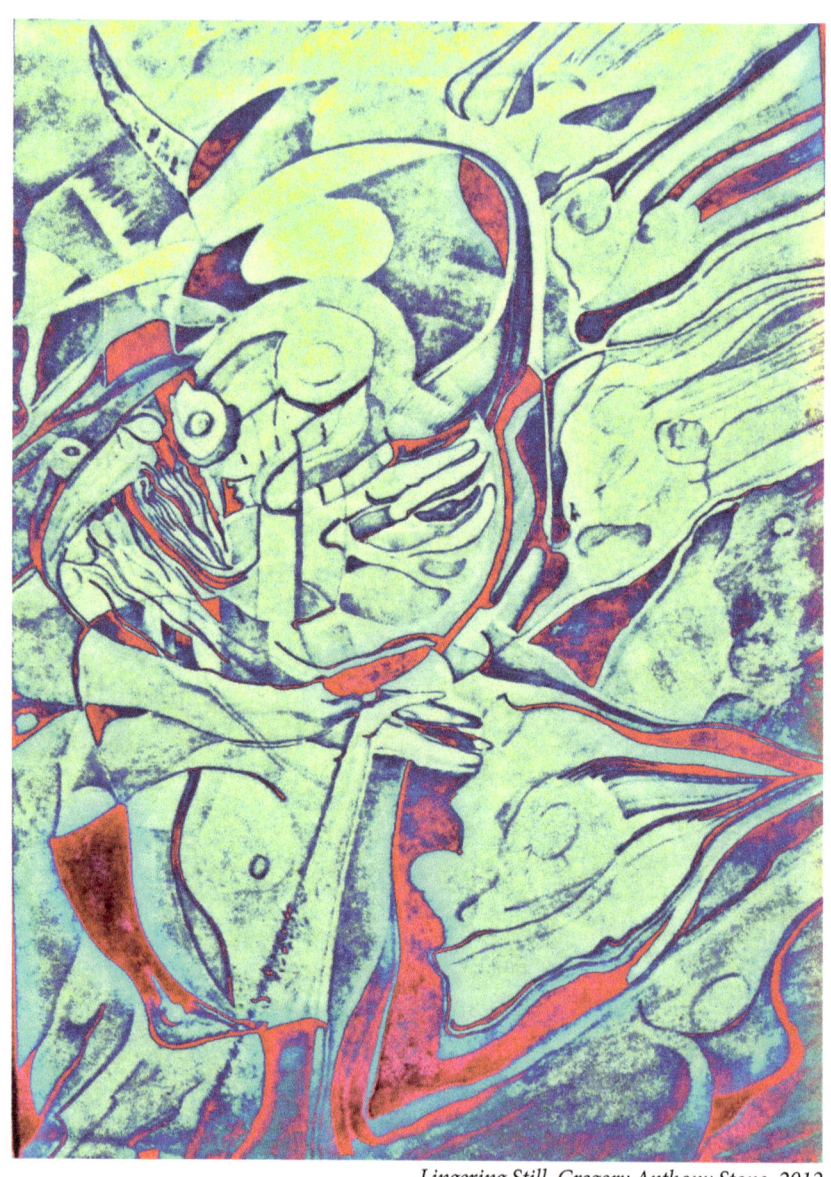

Lingering Still, Gregory Anthony Stone, 2012

ILLEGAL

You have found me waiting just at the border
You, your dogs, your guns, and plastic ties
I want nothing more than
Then to seek and find a better life.
My guide long gone
Just for now
For he will find another group
Seeking the opening
That will allow entrance.
Illegal-
We are not...
Heroin
Cocaine
Weapons
That will overtake you
Ravage and rape your land
And take your innocence...
You are infants
After all.
And so I, we ushered back
To existence is just that
Back to our make-shift houses
(If we're fortunate enough to have one)
Where we watch the tourists
Come and go
A vacation
And we watch as they make their way
In vans passing our children
Our children, offering to trinket or that
As has become our way
Our children, some as young as four
Would approach the vans

Expecting, hoping
They would stop and enable
The tourists to purchase
Their offerings of this or that
The van never stopped
It didn't.
And even though, the tourists had been warned not to
Venture out of the elaborate hotels
With their pools, cabanas, flowing drinks, and an array of varied
Foods
All inclusive-
They came down to our village
Looking for a bargain
A steal.
And if our children were lucky
On this day or that
A tourist, perhaps, taking pity on the
Innocent faces of our children
Would buy what they knew they would
Never need.
It matters little to our young...
Happy that the coins they brought
Home
Would allow us a meal for the night.
More often than not their, our bellies went empty
And tomorrow was another day.
And the ditch, where rain water has made a puddle,
The only beverage they know-
And so it goes
That we look to your borders
Trying to find that bit of life
Far from what is only existence
For us here.
But you are infants
And I, we do not cast blame
It was long ago, or so you say
And such resentment and sadness

Of the possibilities that might have been
Are ignored
Except for us, who wait for your vans
And on occasion-a visit from the straying
Tourists...
the brave...the bold...
The curious...the adventurers...
The pitying...yes...they come.
There is no blame here.
Those explorers of long, very long ago
May not have been your ancestors,
After all.
And like you, they came-
The adventurers...
The bold...
The greedy...
The ravagers...
Rapists...
They came and word spread
Not quickly
But it did.
Some took to the mountains
Making their homes
In recesses and among
Beneath the trees
Far from the ravages, rapes, tortures...
And killing.
And you, as infants, do not speak of this...
Cannot or will not-
In either case, there is no blame
Here.
And the brave, the bold
Who took to the mountains
Escaped...knowing...seeing
What greed can bring.
And so, here, where the Mayans, Incas, Aztecs
Built great structures, worshipped their lands, and

Were happy and content
Would become a memory for us
(Which we speak of often)
And perhaps for you, the infants, who
Read about a time very long ago
When greatness existed
The lessons in your schools, your books
Highlighting our leaders-
Cuauhtémoc, the last Aztec Emperor;
Coanacoch, the King of Texcoco,
Tetlepanquetzal, King of Tlacopan
Motecuhzoma Xocoyotzin -Moctezuma the Young-Montezuma
The great temples and structures
That paid homage to our past-
Lessons that focus on what once was...
But you are infants...
Do you learn, in your many lessons
Of greed, search for gold, acquisition of new land,
Greater treasures, or our religious conversion
And the confusion and pain-
That followed?
The explorers.
In masses, our ancestors, were enslaved
Worked to death
For one cannot survive, live
On meager rations or hours upon hours
Of work without relent and under
Extreme torture and heat of an unforgiving
Sun.
Yes, you see, that was so very, very long ago-
And you are infants still.
You ignore or, in your innocence
Cannot understand-
As we watched
The French, The Spanish, and others
Take and take and never giving back
To the land, our land-

Where we once lived
And ate what the land, our land
Provided
Maize, squashes-pumpkin, butternut
Pinto beans, tomatoes, peppers
Cacao, cotton
We revered nature-
The Jade...water...life...fertility
The Jaguar...a spirit...a guide...powerful...fast
Our writings-
Long, very, very long ago before
The European explorers
Colonization-
Complex logophonetics-
Distinct...
Recording speeches and literature
But, you are an infant and in your innocence
Or in your ignorance, do not care.
We lived in buildings sometimes like lean-tos
Sometimes, adobes
But we lived.
Our temples high-
Our jade sculptures, long since gone
Greed-
And those that came
Built their haciendas
The villagers, our ancestors, far below
Working their fields, building greater structures
Under the watchful eyes of many
Beatings, tortures, deaths
Thousands, tens of thousands of deaths
But, you are an infant.
And so they took and took
Ravaged, raped, and left nothing
There was nothing left to take...
But, truth be told, they left their
Beliefs, their language

As if ours had been wrong, evil-
We became lepers...
And some, many took the mountains-
And there they built and hid
And hide still
Not wishing, wanting for a better
Life.
They live off the land and revere traditions-
And the memory of a time so
Very, very long ago.
But, you are infants
And there is no blame here.
We, exist, survive in our little huts
Some made of wood
If you're fortunate enough
To have one
While we send our children
Unwillingly
To beg, yes, beg
With parched lips and hungry bellies
Some sitting on the dry ground
Waiting, just waiting for the tourist
An infant too-my child waits
Well into the night
And does not realize
That I, we, for we are many
Have hopes of finding that one
Guide who will lead us to a greater
Life
Or at least the chance.

There is no blame here...
You are an infant, after all.
I, have heard, have been given a new name
A new identity
I am an illegal...
My guide gone...
My land ravaged, raped, excavated
Its landscape void of possibilities
Save for the resorts where infant tourists
Lounge by a pool, drinking, taking more food
Than they will eat-
They are infants after all...
They do not know...
That the porter, the housekeeper, the pool boy, the server
Whose ancestors had long ago taken only what the earth would
Provide...
Will one day find his way to a border
Your infant border
And be renamed
An Illegal!

W.N.Y. Winter, Gregory Anthony Stone, 1969

WNY WINTER

I so love the freshly washed linen that is hung
To dry in the gentle breeze and morning sun.
The clothes pins resting in the cloth sack
Suspended just outside the window
Anchored in place on the bricks-
Trousers, shirts, undergarments, and linen
And I would often watch as the pillows
Swayed back and forth
Filled with the fresh air
Like giant balloons
Swaying back and forth.
It is not Winter in WNY-
And so, the laundry is hung
With clothes pins made from two pieces of wood
A spring connecting the two pieces together
And my mother's hands vigorously shaking
The excess water before hanging them all
On the rope that connects from our second floor apartment
To the pole in our back yard.
It is not winter yet in WNY.
It is spring, and I walk down the old, worn,
And creaking steps that will lead me to a side door-
And it begins as I exit
And walk down 67th Street (a very short distance)
And stop at the Fruit and Vegetable Market
Right on the corner of 67th and Bergenline Avenue.
I great the young boy standing just outside the entrance
He is quite familiar
As he stands there each and every day
Making sure, this much I know, that no one
Will take what they will steal any of the
Fresh fruit and vegetables.

I have a nickel...
I fished it out of one of the meters just outside the
Apartment where I lived.
I did this quite often
And often, I was successful
There, on the side street, away from the stares
Glares, really, would not land upon me.
I'd often go from one meter to the next-
Lift up the flap and check
Hoping to find the nickel had not found
Its way into the compartment-
It happened, then, once in a while-
Where, I think, the owner of this car or that one
Was in great hurry and did not fully
Turn the knob that would allow that nickel
To drop.
And so it is, with the nickel in my hand
(Today was not a very profitable one)
And look to see what that nickel will buy me-
An apple, a pear, some grapes, a banana perhaps.
The boy watches me carefully
As I know, expect, he would
And though I have no need to enter
The fruit and vegetable market
I do anyway.
The owners are busily serving the many customers
So they pay me no mind
As I wander about just checking things out
Though I had already decided to save that nickel
And, hopefully, adding more later
Or even tomorrow.
Still, I wander about taking in the smell
Of body odor, sawdust, and rotting fruit-
I'm sure why I found this disgustingly pleasing
But I did!
I exit and make my way south
Passing other fruit and vegetable markets

Clothing stores
Delicatessens
A theater
A parking garage
It is not winter and I can walk
Pass Lobel's across from Roger's
Directly next to Uneeda Television and Stereo
Or enter Woolworth's
I only have a nickel
And with another, I could buy a goldfish
Then what?
I enter anyway
And without any questions, I wonder about
Checking out the bins of undies
Pajamas, sunglasses, toiletries, knick-knacks, socks
I walk up and down aisles-
Just checking things out-
It's something to do
And it's cool inside.
I stop by the food counter with its own register
And watch the people as they come and go
Some just finding a stool
Some just leaving one-
I'm doing neither.
I only have a nickel-
That won't get me a grilled cheese sandwich with French Fries
Of course,
And, I certainly, won't be getting any milkshakes-
Later, perhaps, or even tomorrow
I'll have more luck at the meters.
Back up the
Past the Liquor Store,
Barney's Fine Men's Clothing
(I never understood the need for the word fine though-
Are there stores that sell those that aren't Fine?)
Past the shoemaker's shop
Past the 'Italian Club'

Where men in their crisp white shirts and trousers
Sit on wooden folding chairs
Watching the people passing
I decide to stop in at the record store
That sells small radios, phonographs, and vinyl records...
Petula Clark's record just came out
"Downtown"
I don't have a quarter for it
Come to think of it
I think I'll save that quarter until
I can fish out some more nickels
That will allow me to go back to Woolworth's
Still, I like to look over the records
I hope to buy
One day...
I exit, obviously, the clerk behind the counter
Has had enough of this looking and not buying.
I next enter what many refer to as "The Hippie Shop."
"What scent is that, today?"
I hear someone ask.
"It's ginger snap."
I've to be honest here...
They all smelled the same to me...
It didn't matter what day it was
When I entered, I didn't recognize the smell
It hit my nose and filtered and even lingered
Long after I left...
Overpowering and pungent
It didn't keep me away though...
And besides, I loved the colors of the tie-dye
Shirts, the jeans, the peace signs
Of different colors...
And the people, behind the counters,
Or those helping paying customers
Didn't seem to mind my checking things out
And I did
Quite often, actually.

Back up, what was also called, the Miracle Mile,
Bergenline Avenue
Regardless of the season...
The Miracle Mile!
And back up 67th Street-
Passing the boy, who stands watch over the bins filled
Fruit or vegetables.
(I've heard he gets paid too. He actually gets a quarter a day! I wish I could work and get a quarter. Then, in three days, I could go back to Woolworth's)
It is not WNY in Winter after all
A milkshake just doesn't taste the same in
Winter.
I race up the apartment steps just in time for lunch.
Don't ask me now what I ate...it was long ago...
Now what?
I could go up 67th street (west-it's up hill where the meters call for me)
I stop and check...two nickels!
Finally, reaching Jackson Street
Which runs South and North-
My friend, luckily, is riding her bike
So we take turns...
Never down 67th or any of the other streets that lead to Bergenline Avenue
Braking is rather difficult when you're going down hill
It's the 60's after all-
The Avenue is always busy with people
Going here and there
And the cars and buses wouldn't know enough to stop
No, riding down 67th is not an option.
On Sundays, my mom would always make bacon and eggs
And buttered toast-
"I'm going to church," I say.
Don't know why mom and dad never went-
I did.
Well, most of the time...

There were Sundays, in the Spring and Summer
And even Fall
But seldom in the WNY Winter,
My girlfriend and I would decide to take
Our chances with God
And hoped he wouldn't damn us to hell.
So we'd skip church and walk
The Miracle Mile.
Of course, all of the stores were closed
It was Sunday, after all
(with the exception of the "Italian Club" which, I suppose, wasn't
to be confused with a store).
We would make sure to time ourselves-
Mass runs about an hour
Depending on which priest was giving the Eulogy
And how long he felt the need to preach.
Together, we'd walk down Bergenline Avenue
And simply look into the this store window or another
Not that we could buy anything
If it weren't Sunday
We just liked the idea of dreaming,
Or maybe it was just the fact that doing
The unexpected was exciting-
Sure, guilt often followed,
But at 12, it doesn't last very long.
WNY Winter is a time when all seems to sleep
Or at the very least, slow down.
I'd wear my black and white faux fur coat
That made me look like an undersized cow,
And brave that WNY Winter
Still searching for meter nickels
That I could collect
For a grilled cheese sandwich with French Fries
And a Milkshake
As I made my way down
The Miracle Mile!

ABOUT THE POET

Anna Casamento Arrigo tells of her early days in grammar school when one of her teachers, Mrs. Stern, initiated a deeper and more profound love of poetry. She retells of Mrs. Stern's reading of the poem, "Gunga Din," by Rudyard Kipling and that the teacher began to cry when she reached the half-way point in the poem. She distinctly remembers that stanza;

> The uniform 'e wore
> Was nothin' much before,
> An' rather less than 'arf o' that be'ind,
> For a piece o' twisty rag
> An' a goatskin water-bag
> Was all the field-equipment 'e could find.

It stayed with her and, to this day, vividly sees her beloved teacher, unashamedly and with great love and passion, read those very words and brought them to life for her. It would prove to be the beginning of her love of poetry and all of the emotions that came with it.

While, Anna Casamento Arrigo has written several books, including a memoir, entitled, "Weeds Beneath the Open Meadows," a romance, "The Shadow's Secrets," and a children's book, the first in a series entitled, "Hunter Learns about Honesty," this is her first book of poems.

Anna Casamento Arrigo is often heard reciting poetry, from memory, of some of her favorites including Shakespeare, Edgar Allen Poe, Emily Dickinson, Robert Frost, William Carlos Williams Gwendolyn Brooks, Langston Hughes, and Lawrence Ferlinghetti, just to name a few.

Together with the art works of Gregory Anthony Stone, who Anna Casamento Arrigo says initially inspired her to create the first poem in the book, "All Red," it is one of many, some which are found in this particular collection.

After her stroke, Anna Casamento Arrigo, retired from teaching, where many of her Language Arts' lessons included some of her favorite poems. The memory of that teacher, Mrs. Stern, from her grammar school years and who has long since passed away, still echoing in her ears and urging her, as well as the students she had taught over the years, to find their own passion and their own voice.

ABOUT THE ARTIST

Gregory Anthony Stone, a self-taught Artist, was born May 2,1950 in Jersey City New Jersey and raised in West New York, NJ.

I have lived a long life in my sixty-three years. My biggest regret is the fact that I was not able to continue the path of the scholar, (i.e. higher education). I believe had I continued such a path, I would have been a fine teacher of art. Alas, it was not in the cards for me, and most of my life I worked the "9 to 5" occupations to pay the bills, yet always creating in what little free time I had .I suppose you could refer to me as that proverbial '"Sunday painter "- a moniker I often scoffed at and detested. Now in my sixth decade of life I don't give a damn what moniker is attached to me.

I recall as a small child the first crayon piece I created as a toddler while sitting on the kitchen floor, and the joy it brought my Mum and rest of the family. I guess being an artist started at that precise moment.

On Jul 29,2011 I suffered a spinal injury which left me paralyzed. After a successful spinal operation and months of physical therapy, my hands have come alive again, yet some days are better than others. Walking can still be difficult at times. Before the accident I had started to experiment with digital imagery, and greatly used it in my rehabilitation. It certainly helped me stay sane and kept me away from the darkest of thoughts.

The most important thing in my heart and soul concerning art is the enjoyment of creating. True, at times, it can bring frustration- the artist is never satisfied it seems. And yet one has that need to create. Do it to enjoy it,. Please yourself and never get caught up in the mindset of whether others will like your work. You are putting your soul on display. Sometimes there are bad souls among the good ones. Work at it and forget yourself.

Much of my work has a story, but often I don't offer anything in in the description other than the title. I do intend to correct that. I like to use humor in some pieces and then some echo a darkness. I have had my share of "ups and downs" in this life, suffering from depression and then paralysis (of which I was able to conquer to an extent). Art has always managed to sustain/help me weather the storms. Art is life to me- it's just something I have to do. Try it- you'll like it !

www.ingramcontent.com/pod-product-compliance
Ingram Content Group UK Ltd.
Pitfield, Milton Keynes, MK11 3LW, UK
UKHW020245240426
12048UKWH00026B/1625

9 781633 380028